BEYOND THE PICKET FENCE

27 Stories and Poems about Wildness and Wilderness

A Telling Room Anthology

Introduction

"Wilderness is not only a haven for native plants and animals but it is also a refuge from society. Its a place to go to hear the wind and little else, see the stars and the galaxies, smell the pine trees, feel the cold water, touch the sky and the ground at the same time, listen to coyotes, eat the fresh snow, walk across the desert sands, and realize why its good to go outside of the city and the suburbs."

-John Muir

Themes of wildness abound in the world of children's literature, movies, and stories. In Maurice Sendak's classic, *Where the Wild Things Are*, Max sails deep into the sea of his imagination and becomes a "wild thing," far from society, all while being trapped in the confines of his bedroom walls. In Hayao Miyazaki's beloved *My Neighbor Totoro*, two young girls try to make sense of life while their mother is hospitalized and their father toils at a job in a nearby city when they wander in the woods and into a fantastical journey complete with friendly forest spirits who help and comfort them as they face life as grown-ups for the first time. And in *Winnie the Pooh*, a hundred-acre-wood comes alive with the joys, fears, play, and sadness of a community of animals and one boy who learn, gently, the ways of the world.

In today's world, where are the wild places that young people go to discover who they are and what their place in the world will be? Where do they find a haven to define themselves? What is their inner wild?

Each year, The Telling Room reinvents itself under the auspices of a new theme that permeates our daily writing programs for young people and sets the stage for a new set of ideas, questions, projects, and activities. These themes serve as a way for our community to learn about contemporary life from the perspective of the young people who tackle these questions and ideas in their writing with us. In the past, we have explored themes of belief, neighborhoods, place, food, and more. During the 2013-2014 school year, our theme was WILD. With this theme, we hoped to engage young people in multiple writing projects that explore havens and refuges from society, forbidden places in urban neighborhoods, the abundant wilderness of Maine's forests and coasts, and more.

In these explorations, we'll ask: how and when are we free? Most and least human? Most connected? When are we separate from nature? Why, and how does that impact us? Who or what is the "wild thing" in each of us? Who or what lies beyond our picket fences?

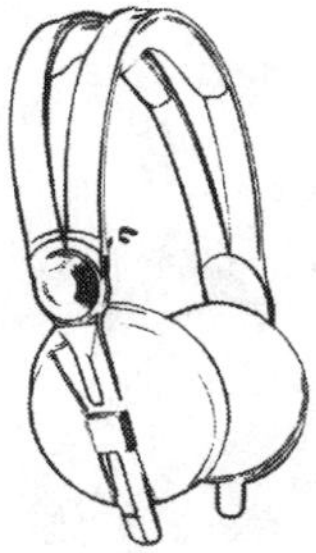

To hear the authors' stories and poems read in their own voices, check out: https://soundcloud.com/tellingroom

TABLE of CONTENTS

PROLOGUE

Henry Spritz

Kenny Lane loved birds. In the summer, the green, shell-speckled rocks that dotted the seashore were home to funny, stilt-legged egrets, frothy seas, and watchful cormorants. In the winter, when the skies were clear of the flashing of wings, the chickadee's quiet call could still be heard in the soft, snow-blanketed woods, a silent guard until the first days of spring.

Kenny Lane watched, he listened, and he observed. In the summer, his mother would call him in to dinner, long after the barnacles and algae had left their mark on him. In the winter, the sticky snow was a bed to those of the light-winged, and sometimes in the quiet evening hush of the woods, Kenny Lane would pretend he was gone, far off, the wind his only competition, no weight strong enough to bring him back to earth.

Kenny Lane lived in Terrencefield, the small town on the coast of Maine known strictly for its fishing, and the annual Terrencefield Fair that was held once a year in the fields on the other side of town. However, to the outsider, Terrencefield was nothing more than a quick pit-stop along the road north, one in a dozen small towns on the coast, and to anyone who looked too quickly, the most they saw of the fine people of Terrencefield was the gloomy old waitress who served sandwiches at the diner on the edge of town, or the loud-mouthed garbage man doing his early rounds in the small hours of the morning, or the hunchbacked bookseller who ran the old, dusty store on Main Street, off to get her morning cup of tea and raspberry scone from the baker's shop down the way.

And so, with the outside world tuned out of the small town lives of the good people of Terrencefield, and the laws of nature, and the circles of life turning well, the hopes of a young boy who loved birds and wished for a miracle were heard, for a moment, and noticed. Then the sun resumed its daily climb in the sky and life continued normally, except that in the autumn months in a small town called Terrencefield, in between the pines and church steeples, and the wind cooing through open windows, a change had occurred, and so set things in motion, like the flap of wings and the gift of flight. A miracle had begun.

* * *

The cabin on Catchers Island was small, but not untidy or poorly made. It was diminutive, yes, but its oak floors and running marble banisters gave light to the extreme wealth that had once inhabited its walls. Mahogany, chestnut, velvet, rich deep tones, grand oriental rugs, faded and worn, golden lamps, and silver dinnerware—all evidence to lives past, lives long past, and buried far down.

The Anglers had been wealthy in the beginning of the twentieth century, businessmen from New York that bought into the logging industry and had hit it big. Joseph Angler (of whom Angler Hall is named) later became the mayor of Whistill, and with a handsome bank account, settled down in the town of Terrencefield after the Second World War when his son, Gregory, had been killed in combat in the Philippines. Aside from Joseph Angler's success, the Angler family's wealth and influence had all but disappeared after the death of Mr. Angler.

The Angler family had owned two estates. One was a sprawling colonial located adjacent to the town church, but had to be put up for sale in the late sixties, simply because the Angler family could not pay the bills. The second was a cabin located on Catchers Island, a small isle across the bay from Terrencefield originally constructed by Mr. Angler to show his support for the fishing industry. For years after Joseph Angler's death, the heirs to the increasingly decreasing Angler fortune resided in the small cottage nestled between the bristling pines and the whipping saltwater wind.

And so the seasons passed, the years, and the time between the first blossoms and the soft quiet snowfalls seemed to blur, passing in and out of reality for the small cabin and its inhabitants. Continually the snow fell softly on a winter night outside the muffled windows, a fire crackled in the quiet, wet dew frosted the doorstep, and drops tracked in on the heels of boots in spring before green vines climbed the shutters along their trellises once more. And all seemed well.

But it had been more than twenty years since the small cabin had seen such living things, and the glass chandeliers that had long burnt out got tired of such dormancy and strung thick cobwebs across the empty rooms. The air came alive with floating dust and spores eager to eat away at the old house. It was winter again, and the heavy drifts of snow clumped outside the house, piling up to overthrow the last manmade obstacle on the island. Icicles dripped from rough roof tiles. It was quiet, and besides the muffled snowfall, a quieter place could never be found. The silence was loud, cold, and sharper than any sting of ice.

CRACK.

The silence was broken.

CRACK. CRACK. CRACK.

And for the first time in over two decades the boots of a man crushed the brittle sticks beneath his feet. The trees swayed and whispered, shaking their branches and showering their paper-thin leaves before him.

CRUNCH. CRUNCH. CRUNCH

The heavy oak door flew open, and the cabin breathed in, sucking in the cold winter air, inhaling the frost, the snow, the water vapor. The man stepped inside, shedding his parka and heavy wool mittens as he went, tossing his hat lazily onto the rack. It fell. He slumped into a chair.

* * *

He rowed away from the island at dawn, in the first hours of morning, when the grey clouds were lazily lifting the blinds and stretching back, and as the sun's golden face peeked over the quiet valley of Terrencefield. As the rooster crowed, the wind chimes glinted and clinked the morning breeze, the pink sky drew roughly on the water's surface, and small ripples stroked the sandy shore.

It was no surprise that as he entered the town, he entered alone. He was no special sight, he carried nothing save a small knapsack thrown across his back, and a stick in his hand, which he tapped and poked across the rocky and uneven ground. It was a good morning, and as the sun drew its sharp breath of warmth over the town, the stirring and the sleepy eyed inhabitants reached over, to grab glasses, hit alarm clocks, shake siblings or loved ones awake; after all, a new day had begun for Terrencefield, and woe to anyone who would miss it.

SPARROWS

Omar Raouf

When I was nine, I had a sparrow that lived in a small cage by the window. One day, I left the cage door open and the sparrow flew out the window. I never thought I would see the sparrow again, but later that day he came back. My grandmother had thrown breadcrumbs in the garden and he had come back to eat them. It's almost impossible to tell one sparrow from the rest, but I knew he was my sparrow. There were many little things that were different about my sparrow from all the other sparrows, but I can't really tell you what they were. I just knew he was mine.

Trying to recognize one sparrow from another for humans is like trying to tell apart the two factions of Islam if you're not a Muslim. For our family, however, in 2006, the blind hatred between two religious groups was terrifying. People in both groups were killed, whether they were involved in the conflict or not. One blind-minded group wanted to avenge what they thought was a terrible offense against them over 1,000 years ago. They believed they still needed to avenge this offense. That's a long time to hold a grudge. Therefore, my father decided we had to leave Baghdad. He said we had no choice.

Leaving the place you grew up in makes you feel like a tree being pulled, roots and all, from its environment. Then you get planted in a different place. I can clearly recall the day I got into the GMC with my family to leave Baghdad, perhaps forever, I thought then. I was leaving behind nine years of laughing, crying, and playing with family and friends; leaving behind the smell of my aunt's sweet flatbread and me eagerly awaiting my small piece. I remembered my grandmother breaking open olive green cardamom pods and adding them to our small cups, called *istikan*, and then pouring the red tea over them. The cups are not at all like European cups. *Istikan* are shaped like upside-down bells. I remember the echo of the spoon hitting the edges of the cups as everyone stirred their tea. The sound is still ringing in my head.

This is only one of many memories of my life in Baghdad. I will tell you more as they occur to me. The time got slower as we walked closer to the GMC. Our feet knew what our hearts felt and they didn't want to go either. As I turned around, my eyes fell on my dad. I saw him brushing a tear off his cheek, and I felt his sadness and love for our old home. I felt his sadness for being forced to leave and love for the family, friends, and the streets where he grew up and spent his best days. I was shocked, watching my dad. I looked at the rest of my family and saw we shared the same look of sadness and love.

As we rode out of Baghdad, I sat in the backseat looking through the windows, trying to see as much as I could of my home, a huge city, as the sunlight hit my eyes. The car carried me further from home. Everything blurred into lines of lights, buildings, and people, all flashing by like the pages in a book being turned so quickly that I couldn't read the words.

When we stopped in the traffic I felt better because I

could recognize the buildings and give them a last look, I could say goodbye. The line of traffic was so long that I couldn't see the light when it turned green. The only way I could tell was when I saw the brake lights of the cars ahead of us turn off. That meant we'd move forward and further. It was like this over and over again until we left the city and got on the highway, where we moved faster. Then, after a short time on the highway, I couldn't see the city that we had left behind and couldn't tell when we would stop.

I kept asking my dad how long it would take until we reached our new home. He told me, "In seven or eight hours, son." As we went further on the highway, the landscape became a desert. I leaned my head back, but there was nothing left to see. Asking myself all sorts of questions about today and yesterday, I fell asleep.

When I woke up, the sun was about to set. The sunset in the wild was the best thing I had ever seen; I didn't want to close my eyes, even for a second, so that I could enjoy every moment of that view. It was something I had only seen in cartoons and never thought I would see in reality. It was one of the best moments that I have ever enjoyed with my family. It seemed to ease our minds and lighten the pressures that we were feeling. The sun kept moving until that blazing orange sank behind the horizon. That was when darkness covered the wild, and all I could see were clusters of stars, like candles that light the sky.

I could hear my dad and the driver talking about "the border," but I didn't know what it was or what it would look like. Then my dad asked my mom for the passports, another subject I didn't understand, even though they were speaking in Arabic, my first language. My mom had prepared some food for the car ride and told me that as soon as we reached our new home she would cook my favorite meal. While I ate my sandwich, I could see the sand particles reflecting the moonlight out over the desert.

All night we drove closer to the border, but we were still on the very dangerous highway. It was almost sunrise as I looked through the window to tell where we were and what was going on around us, even though I couldn't recognize the places. After I woke up, I saw this weird dark shape on the side of the road. Some smoke was coming out of it. It was visible because the orange sun was once again in the sky. I could see a shape that had once been an automobile, but I had never seen one burn before.

Just after this scene I looked at my dad. I could see he was getting more worried. I don't remember my dad's face looking relaxed at all during the trip. I had many questions that I was anxious to ask, but every time I looked at my dad I stopped myself because I didn't want to bother him with my silly questions. There were other cars on the highway and I could tell that they were fleeing Baghdad, too, from the suitcases piled on top of the car or stacked in the back window. I felt better knowing that other people were leaving and that we were not the only sparrows.

After a few more hours, I could see several long rows of cars ahead of us. I began trying to count the number of cars ahead of us so that I would know how long it would take us to reach the border. I could see that we would have to wait for about ten cars to go before it was our turn. As I was counting, I stuck my head out the window a little bit so that I could see more clearly. When my mom saw me, she told me to pull my head back in the car quickly. American and Iraqi soldiers and snipers manned this checkpoint, armed to their teeth. They got suspicious of anyone leaving their cars or appearing out of the windows, suspecting that they might intend to shoot at them. Their primary strategy was to shoot anything that moved out of place.

My dad had prepared all of the paperwork, and I could see that he was less worried than he had been, but our driver was getting increasingly nervous because he was the one who was usually responsible for taking care of the paperwork. Finally, we got to the checkpoint. It was dark outside, but there was some light in the checkpoint building. The driver left the car with the paperwork. Some time later, he came back and asked my dad to go inside with him for a security check, and as my dad left with the driver, two policemen came up to our car holding flashlights and machines that beeped. They checked the car.

Inside, my dad had to give his fingerprints and put his face to a machine that would take his eye print. However, my dad's vision was deteriorating and his retina was damaged, and the police got suspicious because they did not find him on their computers. He had to stay there for a while. The driver came back and told us what happened. My mom was praying. I was even more worried than she was because I didn't understand what was happening or what they might do to him. Fortunately, our fears were not realized. My dad came back to the car unharmed and we were able to pass the checkpoint.

We finally reached Syria, passed through Damascus, and were approaching Tartus. While we were still on the road, we stopped at a restaurant and I tasted the Syrian bread and food for the first time. I was hungry so I had no choice but to eat, and after I finished I realized that it wasn't bad to try new foods. While we were eating our lunch, I listened to the people speaking around me. I could tell what they were talking about, but I couldn't speak the same way; they were speaking much faster than I was used to. I was afraid to talk because I felt as though I would reveal myself as a stranger, someone who didn't belong.

We got back on the road, and the closer we got to my new home the more the things I saw excited me. Tartus is a beautiful city lying next to the Mediterranean Sea, surrounded by valleys with rivers cutting through it. I could see olive trees on the steppes and covering the sides of the mountains. As we drove, I wondered what school I would be going to and what it would look like. Would I still be able to chase a ball? Would I easily make new friends? Would I ride my bike in my new neighborhood? All these thoughts hit me in the head. For a moment I felt sad. I had never worried about being a stranger to a place before and once I did, I knew I would always miss the old things I loved. Suddenly, my view of the whole experience of this new city changed.

My worries, however, ended up being fleeting. Once I got to know the city that would be my new home—the buildings, the houses, the mosques and the churches—I learned that it wasn't that different from my old city. What I really liked was the view and smell of the sea. The water reflected the sun's light, like the sand did in the moon's light in the desert. I would learn to love this place as much as my former home in Baghdad. Sparrows are very adaptable; they can be happy anywhere. Maybe they have no choice.

IN THE BLIND

Noah Williams

He seemed happiest afield, and never before had he seemed so immersed in reality. At home, he could stare off into space for hours while children climbed all over him, and my mother tried to talk to him about some scheduling. His belief that nothing was as it seemed drove him into such deep, swirling, and mysterious places within his own head that perhaps it was truly impossible for him to remain present at all times. But in a duck blind, wearing an enormous olive green overcoat and with a shotgun in his the crook of his arm, he was all there. His eyes never left the birds as they circled overhead.

He'd planned the decoy spread thoughtfully, placing the foam replicas in a pattern that made our stretch of shore seem more appealing to ducks overhead. My brother Gene and I would stay in the blind with whichever dog had accompanied us on this trip, watching him carefully place each decoy in a half circle, leaving an open area for the ducks to land directly in front of us. We sat there, in frozen silence for what seemed like days, punctuated only by the faint whistle of various species of waterfowl passing overhead.

He could name them all: mallards, teal, widgeon, black duck, and the odd pintail, but sadly his powers of identification were woefully unnecessary in the marshes of southern Maine. He lifted the call to his lips and gave a loud hail call, signaling to the group above that we ducks below wanted their company. They circled again, lower this time, and as they wheeled over us the third time we could pick out the green heads of individual male mallards in amongst the drab brown hens. The dog whined, and flicked her head from the ducks to my father, who, with one hand motion, silenced the animal and then motioned for one of us to hold her still.

A fourth time, the wary group circled us above, and my father gave them encouraging chuckles. Suddenly, they started to bank, and the whole flock of them started to slide through the air into the "pot" my father had created for them to land in amongst the decoys. As the black shadows of the birds turned into the rising sunlight, their green heads glistening in the frosty dawn, my father breathed, "Take 'em."

Gene and I sprang from the hard wooden seat of the blind, the barrels of our guns pushing away the sparse web of branches that concealed us. The birds stalled in midflight, their wild brown eyes glittering in surprise. I distinctly remember looking over the barrel of my Remington 870, which my great grandfather had given to my father, and watching the drake mallard flare upward, his gray belly pale against the orange horizon. I remember, too, the bang and shock of the gun going off, the duck folding in mid air, almost like a paper balloon when the winds turn it inside out, and the limp body plummeting into the dark water below.

Gene had shot twice, I had shot once, and each of us had killed a bird. The dog plunged into the icy water, grateful for this opportunity to do something. My father was laughing as he reached over and clapped us heavily on the backs. When the dog brought the first duck back, my father took it from her mouth and sent her out again, and handed the bird across Gene to me. "That one's yours," he said quietly, his face beaming, his mouth in the thin, closed lip smile that was so characteristic of him whenever he shared what he believed was an important moment.

I held the little body in my hand, amazed at the extreme beauty of the pencil gray underbelly and patches of iridescent blue on the wings. They had seemed bigger flying in over the decoys. Two thin trickles of blood flowed out of the duck's breast, and dropped onto the floor of the blind. I turned it over in my hand and admired the yellow bill, and dark green head. I gently stroked the duck's delicate cheek, ruffling the feathers, and as carefully as if the bird had been sleeping, I pulled down on the fuzzy gray eyelid and exposed the dark brown eye that moments before had been burning with the intensity of life.

"He's a beautiful bird, Ernest," my father said quietly. I just smiled and nodded my head, still in awe of the bird in my hands.

My father knew that not everyone loved to kill things as much as he did. And he also knew that if you were to take children hunting, you must let them have their own moments, completely separate from the group, from the hunt, from everything, and absorb the experience they've just had. I never took killing lightly like Gene did, and I never embraced it with the enthusiasm of my father.

My father had tried so hard to instill in me the fact

that all life had meaning, and death did, too, so that hunting and killing were not the same. These ideas made me stop and pay solace to this incredible animal. My father had been taught as a child that killing was wrong, yet as he grew older he said, it seemed as if that became less true, and for some period in his life there was no worth at all to a living being.

But where do you draw the line? Does a woodchuck's life have less meaning than a human's? How do you assign meaning to something so abstract? What is worth something, and how much, and what has value?

A photograph captured the day. All three of us are sitting on the tailgate of the truck. My father is in the middle wearing an enormous smile on his unshaven face. He has a hand on each of our shoulders; I am on his right, and Gene is on his left. Gene and I are holding our guns crooked in our arms across our chests so that the muzzles are pointing skyward. Gene is holding his duck by the neck and grinning with predatory pride, something my father would later come to regret. I am holding my duck in two hands, supporting its head. Its wings hang down below its body, covering my other hand. Although I am smiling, it is not a smile of pride or excitement like Gene's or my father's, but a quieter one.

BEYOND THE PICKET FENCE

Taryn Brennan

I. Venus Flytrap
He fled the despotic bog, his birthplace, in favor of the bright forest just beyond the picket fence. The trees whispered their comfort and protection; songbirds flitted amongst their boughs. Lost, an alluring aroma below offered him guidance. He found her, mouth open, nectar succulent. Enthralled, he landed amid teeth and darkness swallowed him whole.

II. Red Delicious
She is encased in a thin, red veil hiding bruises just below her surface. She falls and withers; her form collapses into itself, core exposed. The soft ground absorbs her, its ravenous soil ripping the nutrients from her rotting figure. A seedling breaks through the crust; the earth shifts, striving to replace death with life.

III. Ants
Rich dirt protests as mandibles shred it into black ribbons and small, six-legged creatures permeate its more porous surfaces. They gut the earth's insides and craft long winding highways. Their blood constructs a castle and guards stand by. The ground moves; millions of ruthless beings

overrun a decaying fruit, engulfing the sphere—a microcosmic globe.

IV. Black Widow

She is cloaked in sleek black, accented by a red redolent of her victims; she is a femme fatale. She stalks her web provocatively, waiting for a mate or insect to stumble into it—both are potential prey. Her venom leaves one gasping for air, its body writhing in agony as she gleefully watches nearby.

V. Mushrooms

Rain had saturated the earth, inspiring bright hooded figures to appear in the foliage. Raindrops danced on their caps and rinsed their stalks clean of the dirt clinging to them. The earth's lithe fingers intermingle with those of a corpse long forgotten. They reach toward the dark, low-lying clouds yearning for the sunlight behind them.

LET ME TELL YOU ABOUT HER

Maimuna Hassan

I was born in 1995 in a small village in Kenya. I grew up in a large mud house, which was really three separate houses with metal roofs, plus a pen for the goats, and a fence surrounded all of it. There were two entrances, one for animals and one for us. Each hut had a bedroom: one for my parents, one for my siblings and me, and one for guests who stay.

My mom would wake us up at six every morning to go to school. Our school was blue on the outside and pink inside and had a thousand students. It was diverse, with white kids, Sudanese, Congolese–but most of the kids were Somali. I started school when I was six years old.

One cold, windy foggy day, I was walking home from school and it started to rain and thunder. I ran to my neighbor's house. The thunder scared me. Every time I heard it, I imagined that someone was burning and the thunder was their moaning. When the storm stopped, my dad came to take me home, calling me to come outside. "Close your eyes," he said, and then, "Surprise!"

I opened my eyes and there was the biggest surprise of my life: a little goat. She was black and white and had pretty brown eyes. I named her Fatoush, after my best friend who had died earlier that year.

One day when my mom was in another country and I was staying with my cousin, I wanted to take my goat for a walk. It was so hot no one went to work, and everybody wanted to be outside. It was like a national holiday. I saw my cousin taking his goats out. I asked him if I could tag along. He said I could, so I did and brought Fatoush. As we walked, another girl joined us, too. When we got to the grassy place, my cousin told me that he and the girl would watch the goats and I could relax. I started playing with my favorite Barbie doll and forgot about Fatoush.

After a while, I could sense quietness. I looked up, and I saw my goat running toward the forest. I ran to my cousin. "Fatoush is gone! Fatoush is gone!" But he was too busy chatting with the cute girl who'd come along with us to pay any attention to me. I started running after Fatoush, and then I heard a strange sound coming from the direction she was headed.

It was a hyena. I grabbed Fatoush, picked her up, and as the hyena got closer, I held her tightly. The hyena was right in front of me. I thought I was going to die. Suddenly, an arrow struck the hyena, killing it. The man who shot it smiled at me and walked away without a word. My cousin ran toward me and took me home.

The next morning, I saw my aunt taking the goats out this time, and Fatoush and I went along with her. As soon as we got to the grassy place, I played with my Barbie again, and again I let my goat wander. I heard my aunt scream, and then she screamed again. I ran to her and saw a hyena eating Fatoush. I just stared. My aunt grabbed my arm and started to gather the other goats with me in tow, but then we noticed the hyena moving toward us. Suddenly, she pulled out a knife and threw it. The hyena fell, dead.

Five years later, my cousin married the girl he was flirting with. A year after that they had a baby girl, and they named her Fatoush.

UNCAGED

Marissa Heffernan

A cat curls within my chest, occupying the space between my heart and lungs. She's not a domestic tabby, preening glossy fur and sheathing delicate claws. She's not a pet at all. She's feral. Shaggy grey fur coats her lithe frame, all sinew and grit and bone, and her eyes blaze green fire, hissing sparks of pure wildness. She slumbers there, inside the warm hollow of my body, dozing lightly and waiting for the brisk scent of forest air to flow over constantly alert olfactory sensors. Odors of leaf litter and sun blend, creating an aroma of freedom, rousing her from sleep.

Her whiskers twitch as I take the first few steps along a dirt trail leading to a mountaintop. Her ears flick as I pass through the quiet murmurs of the trees. Her tail stirs the air in rapid anticipation as the forest surrounds me. Every step onto fallen needles, over tree roots, and through streams excites her muscles twined under a hide thickened by tumbles and whipping branches. But the wild beast inside me does not arch her back and fully wake up until my boots start to clamber up to higher elevations.

When I get to a rocky ledge, I remove my boots and edge my toes over the precipice, examining the way they hover over the forest below. I feel the breeze curl underneath them. Then, my animal bursts free from the carrying cage of my ribs, no longer restrained by the city. I shut my eyes and throw my arms wide to experience the world from a new perspective.

When I open them again, they scuttle across the tapestry of tree trunks and undergrowth, picking out a jumpy squirrel and a bold-colored bird from the general blur of nature rushing by. My claws prick the springy earth and jolt me forward at a greater pace. Air curves around my pointed face, dousing my senses with information and plastering fur closer to my streamlined body. When a nutty musk filters in, igniting my most primal instinct, I extend my claws fully, ending my forward momentum in one jarring turn. My tail lashes furiously to retain equilibrium.

Sinking close to the earth, I narrow my gaze until only a chipmunk, oblivious to my presence, fills my vision. I tense my hind legs until every fiber inside quivers with the rushing lust for the hunt. My prey freezes, instincts alerting it, just as I leap forward. I land squarely on the squealing rodent. Blood beats under my paw, the chipmunk's trembles running up my leg. I flex my claws, and then the desire to kill leeches from me as quickly as it appeared.

I settle back on my haunches and lift the offending paw. The chipmunk flees for freedom. The excitement lies in the chase, in the headlong race, and not in the catch. Dropping low and twisting to carve out an indentation in the ground, I wrap my tail around tucked-in paws and nestle my chin atop the pile of fur. My eyes fall to slits, and my ears remain vigilant. As I blend into the backdrop, the smaller creatures of the forest return to their scuttling. In leafy penthouses, birds gossip frantically, each competing for the juiciest bit of melody, while chipmunks nervously skirt my area, going about their foraging with anxious steps and constant glances at me. As the forest returns to full volume, I drift absently, appreciating the sigh of the wind and the kiss of the sun until, suddenly, every grey hair along my spine bristles into action.

Green orbs flash as my muscles clench in a practiced movement. I slip razors from their sheaths in my paws and assess every angle for the threat, the unnatural quiet pressing down on my eardrums. I strain minute tendons, searching the mountainside, until harsh voices grate against my overextended senses. The shock holds the same affect as a bolt of lightning, propelling me a foot in the air. A snarl, halfway between a hiss and a meow, rips along my vocal chords.

In the same second, I return to my human form. Standing above tree line, I am just in time to offer a wan smile to the busily chatting group of twenty-somethings that just shattered my wild sanctuary. Their conversation and laughter pollutes the mountaintop, and I feel the social restraint their arrival brings creeping towards me, drawing the cat within to twine sullenly around inside me. Not yet willing to cage my wildness entirely, I turn my steps to the descent. Every pace back toward civilization acts as a tranquilizer to my feral feline. By the time I reach the parking lot, the cat slumbers once more inside my chest, curled softly around my nature-based soul, guarding it from the dangers of the city until I can be free once more.

ATOP A WINDY PEAK

Ethan Boardman

The day is sunny and warm.
The birds chirp as I look over the gorgeous view.
I see dozens of lakes surrounded by hills and coated with pine trees.
The wind pops up and snatches my breath, stunning me as I begin to climb.

As I clear the tree line, the wind is like a giant fist.
It wants to smash me into the ragged rocks and punch me over the cliff.
Katahdin is trying to blow me off his back like a grizzly bear swatting away pesky fleas.

I scale the bald face of the boulders, looking for crevices.
I reach the top of a lonely peak.
Oh, how I wish the top of that peak was the top of the mountain!
Alas, the trek continues, sapping my endurance and my eagerness to reach the top, in the ever-increasing gale.

I know I must finish.
Slowly, I trudge on, against the wind's will.
Finally, finally, I reach the top.
In four hours.

I feel amazing up there, on the top of Maine.
I stare down the cragged rocks forming the steep cliff.
A large rock shields me from the mighty wind and tranquility rolls off the summit.
The mountain has accepted me, and we are at peace.

SCATTERED SEEDS

Rasha Usif

I used to live in a house in Darfur where the roof was red, near my grandmother's farm. It had two windows and more than eight brick steps leading up to it. We had three rooms. My grandmother and my mother had their own rooms, but I shared mine with my brother, Esam. We had another house next to this house. The windows were big, and if I was in one house, I could see my brother in the other. They were very close together. My grandmother wasn't comfortable when there were many people in the house. She was always worried something could happen. She knew things like that–she knew guns would come, and bombs, and the place would be turned upside down on her.

My house was a three-minute run from our farm. I didn't like the red brick steps in front of the house. I fell down them sometimes because the rain made them slippery. The last time I was in Sudan when it rained, the water came up to my shoulder. When that happened, men and women in the town dug trenches. Sometimes my grandmother directed the water to the farm, and sometimes it just ran out and away. When it was the dry season, I would go see my father in Khartoum, which was a three-day train ride away. My father works at a company there, in an important position, and every day a brown car would come and pick him up and take him to work. Sometimes my mom would miss us and tell us to come home–to return to the farm.

I loved the farm so much. The thing I liked best about it was that we grew a lot of peanuts. I also loved watching my grandmother and the cow doing the plowing. The cow knew how to plow, and my grandmother walked in front of her, came back to hit the cow once, ran in front again, and the cow followed and pulled the plow. It looked funny when she was in front and the cow was behind her, instead of the other way around. When the plow flipped the soil over, it looked like someone stirring it. When the cow finished plowing, people came into the field and sprinkled all kinds of seeds, like red and black beans, into the ground, hoping for a good growing year. I liked scattering seeds, too. We used our feet to tuck the seeds in and close the earth around them.

My grandmother would often say around the farm, "Watch! Because next time you're going to be doing it!" I learned so much from my grandmother. She was tall and strong, full of hope and determination, and still young. The farm was a gift from her mother. She felt very close to the farm. It was the one thing her mother left her, and she loved it. She was the one in charge. She had a lot of people to do what she told them to do. About fifty people came everyday to work on the farm. Some of them were related to us, and some were close friends. She trusted them and wanted them to work for her. Sometimes she would go help at other farms, and other times people from other farms would help her.

Sometimes my grandmother and I rode our horses to the farm, especially if my mom was already there.

We never went straight there on the horses. She took us in big loops, around and around, because sometimes she was tired of working and wanted to have a little fun. Every time we rode we passed a big, green tree. She told me that her grandmother and her mother were born under that tree, and she was too. They were like a part of the tree–they came from its roots.

My grandmother told lots of stories like that. She told my mother about how she learned to grow seeds by herself. My mother takes messages of hope and strength from my grandmother's stories, because she thinks that one day everything will happen just as her mother says it will. My grandmother just knows things.

* * *

A day came when my brother and I were standing next to our farm gate when we saw some people on horses holding guns coming straight into town. They were tall and were wearing women's dresses and scarves on their faces. They got close to us and then started shooting people down. At that time I was really afraid that they might shoot me too, but my grandmother and mother came and took us to the house. My mother moved my grandfather's bed away from where it usually was, and there was a hole in the floor. Later, I learned that the hole had always been there, always for hiding children when bad people came. My brother, mother, and I got inside the hole.

My grandmother did not go in it because she knew, from many other times, what these people wanted to take from the town, and she knew how to talk to them. Once or twice a year, they would come, their faces covered. My grandmother knew some of these people. One of them used to live in the town with her, and she recognized him when his scarf fell off his face. Half of them would come to the middle of the town and talk about the town's food and animals because they did not have houses to live in, food to eat, or animals of their own. The other half of the people would go to the houses around the edges of town and steal from them.

We were down there in the hole for almost an hour hearing people call their children and mothers. It took about six or seven hours for the bad people to steal what they wanted, but the townspeople decided not to let them take their animals and food and they tried to fight them back. They caught one of the people on the horses but the others ran away. Then at last my grandmother came and opened the door for us to get out. It was around seven o›clock or seven thirty when the fighting finished–we'd been in there since noon.

The next morning the people came back to the man that they had caught to ask him why the bandits had done what they did, and who had told them to come to our town and steal from us. He told the people that he was working for someone, but he would not say who that person was or where he was. My grandmother was there, and she decided it was time for her to speak. She asked the man if he wanted to live or die. If he wanted to live, she said, he had to show them where the person he worked for was.

For the rest of the day we waited for the man to tell my grandmother who the man was that he worked for, and after hours and hours he decided to tell. When the people finally found his accomplice, the people in our town made him pay money and bring back all the stuff he had taken from us, and my grandfather told the pair of men that if they ever returned to that town again, it would be their last day. They believed it, too, because my grandparents are the kind of people everyone listens to and respects, even bandits. They have a kind of strength that seems as though it cannot be stopped.

* * *

Days after the bandit left, my grandmother was walking to work when a bomb exploded near her. She flew to the other side of the house. The people ran to my grandmother and helped her, before coming to tell us what had happened. They took her to the hospital and looked after us. This was because of my grandmother's kindness and care for everyone. It was her turn.

My mother, my brother, and I went to the hospital to see her. It was hard for us to see her, our strong grandmother, in the hospital. She was there for almost six months. My mother sometimes slept by her side. On the days when my mother was in the hospital, a person from our town came to be with us, until the next day, and then another person came. My grandmother's farm stayed the way it was because the people loved her and didn't want to her to lose it.

My grandmother got out of the hospital, but she never found out who had put that bomb there. I know that if she had, she would have taught the bad person a thing or two about how to behave. She does not walk the same way she used to: strong, like the tall branches of the tree that she had been born under, and firm, like the plants that grew from the seeds she'd scattered so hopefully; but she still works on her farm, and still she knows things.

It has been almost nine or ten years since my mother has seen her mother, but this March, she will go back to Sudan and see my grandmother after so many years. I hope my mother will carry my grandmother's messages of hope and strength back to her.

A STRIKE OF STARS

Cameron Jury

We looked up,
up into the sky.
We looked at the stars,
searching for what was inside those shining dots of light.
We imagined their movement.
We stood listening,
listening to peace and nothingness;
the sounds of the black night.
We were hopeful.

One came,
a shooting star flying across the night sky.
Daring to stand out,
to challenge the moon for attention.
Calling for our amazement, it was
brave enough to come out of its hiding place
in space.
We held our breath.

It seemed even the crickets stood silent, watching,
not believing it was real.
I shut my eyes tightly.

The image of the star
shooting across the sky

played in my mind
as I made a wish.
A wish for peace,
a wish for more miracles,
a wish for the world.

We stared back up.
Our cold fingers shot up into the air,
pointing out more and more.
With many came power.
It was like a strike,
a strike of stars
against being hidden, against being lonely.
None of us moved.

We had become one with the night.
We were all stars, united with the blackness.
Together, we held hands.
Soaring across the sky,
we joined them
and didn't stop flying until the sun awoke,
and the day came.

WHALEBACK

Anna Mitchell

The red suburban crept along the sea foam blanketed pavement, carrying us like a faithful steed into battle. The wind blew at an unruly pace, lifting wave after wave into the somber sky. The tires rolled. The ocean rolled.

Buoys and traps were strewn around us, as if left behind by a child called to dinner from his play, forgotten with the promise of something more significant. I turned my head, and was met by the once menacing view of the ocean, a set of stormy, evergreen eyes, perplexed as the titanic body jived a tango. And in a heartbeat, again, the sight made me crumble. It was fickle that day, in the tradition of ages.

We skidded to a salty, rain-driven halt. I savored the strange sense of calm that settled over us. It muffled the howl that rocked the vehicle. A steady hand reached for the handle, shook it so as to loosen its age-clenched grasp, and pushed outward against the force of the rain, thus opening the door. Greeting the wind, we were consumed by the raging storm.

Picking our way to the shore, it was clear this visit would last no longer than the moment one of us children began to cry. Maybe merely a whimper would inspire a departure in this treachery, for it felt as if the tautness of the moment could be plucked, echoing the enchantments of naivety and dissipating into the extremity of our little minds.

It was called Whaleback, our lithic destination, named for its appearance. We had adorned our sun-bleached curls with our flowered dresses and we seemed out of place. We were too much concentrated light, when this day seemed in closer relation to the night.

The four of us crawled with vigor as far as the wind permitted, and then we stood. We stood tall, braced by our solid souls, braced by the strength of what we are raised to become. Free. And all around us was chaos. The beautiful, savage kind that you can't help but admire, like heaven and hell, and everything in between.

DEFYING CONFORMITY

Madolyn Connolly

Prejudice reigned upon my Irish skin
Freckles smudged by the hand of the congregation
Clothes pressed by a fiery rule
Iron chipping against iron

I could smell the church on her breath
As she leaned in
Air pierced by one-sided remarks
Her blinders of faith stiff against withering flesh
The foggy whites of her eyes reflecting the text
Pupils becoming crossed
Refusing to join
The mindless mobs who cram into tarnished
oak benches
And drink the rosie water
From a sacred dust-caked sink

They say my book on evolution is a sin
For God forbid,
It preaches diversity, knowledge, and open-mindedness
No longer bound tightly by the corruption
With backs aching from guilt
And knees bruised from stone-cushioned kneelers
No long skirts can hide it
For the stitches snap at the seams

Exposing ankles shackled by money
And a ball slogging behind with greed
Chains become tangled
Morals still lost
While searching for a key
Which lies
Outside the walls of the church

O ACADIA!

Mary McColley

O Acadia! Acadia!
Your wild, heaving sea
Broils white with foam and spray–
And ever may it be.

Like horses fueled by anger
The thunderous waves avail,
But never shall they conquer rock,
Though in tumult do they rail.

The gath'ring noise! The leaps of height!
The beauty of the foam!
Oh, surging waves, what power lies
In the moon-pull of your home.

Such shades of color as only seen
In thought, the sea puts on.
Deepening blues, and slightest greens,
And grays like stormy dawns.

The riveting cascade of ocean
Against the watered rock
Is thick and pure–and glistening–
A key to beauty's lock.

Rain of light, of foam, don't cease!
Your music fills the air
With orchestrated slap of stone
And breeze, from who-knows-where.

O Acadia! Acadia!
This wonder fills my mind
Such pow'r–such blues–such sky so free–
Such is God's, not mine.

THE ROCK

Nick Hutchins

The cool ocean breeze blows through my hair and the waves crash on the hard ocean bottom as I slip my body into the wetsuit and paddle out. The strong rip pulls me closer and closer to the huge slab of earth sticking up like a skyscraper right in the middle of the lineup. The waves are coming in fast now, smashing into the rock only a few feet away from me, creating a splash as high as a house. For every foot I paddle away from it the rip takes me two feet back. As the frigid salt water splashes against my face all I can think about is not hitting the rock.

I'm lying here on my surfboard but no part of me is still–my arms are moving so fast that I feel like I've done a thousand push-ups, my hands are digging so deep they are practically scraping the bottom, and I am panting so hard I feel like a dog after running too much on a hot summer day. The only thing keeping me from giving up is the razor sharp slab of earth sticking up from the white sandy beach.

But at last I realize I can't win against the current and I stop paddling. I put my arms up on my surfboard and let the current drag me closer to the rock. When I hear the sound of my board scraping against it, I close my eyes. I just lie here hoping, praying that the rock doesn't take my flesh with the board. I feel that I am not able to do a single thing more. My body and my surfboard are at the will of the ocean.

Then the scraping stops. I open my eyes. I am on the other side, sloshing softly back into a new current, heading for a breaker. I breathe again and take in the ocean's strength because I still want to catch one of these monster eight footers into shore.

IN A TINY PLACE

Annick Umutoniwase

Without the sound of the water, it was a beautiful, quiet place surrounded by yellow flowers. I had a perfect view of it from inside the window. It was long, a little bit higher, and tiny, but just right for me. It was my favorite place to go, because it was the one place where I could convince myself that I could swim. My parents and other elders in my house were always worried that my sisters and I would catch some dangerous bacteria in that place. All the water that came around the edges of the house and down from the roof was dirty.

I never cared much about anything I did back then. I told myself that a ten-year-old was still too young to care about her actions and the consequences that came with them. I was just a little girl without responsibilities. I remember one time when the sky changed from sunny to gray. There was lightning and the thunder was booming. The power of the raindrops made big holes in the sandy ground. But I knew that as long as it was raining I didn't care about how bad the storm was, because there would be a lot of fresh water in my place. During the middle of a rainstorm was the perfect time to be there.

My nanny told my sisters and me not to go outside because it was dangerous, but I always thought she didn't want me to go because the water was dirty. She was being protective because she loved us so much. She was a kind and generous woman who treated us like we were her own daughters. She liked to tell us stories whenever we came home from school. Funny ones, sad ones, and sometimes stories about what it was like when she was our age. I would listen to her stories, but I couldn't keep my mind there. Standing in the living room, looking through the window, watching a lot of water running down in my favorite place, I snuck out from the back door and went there because I couldn't be patient and stay in the house during that good soaking rain.

All I ever did in my tiny place was go into it with my back facing the ground, and my face toward the sky. But this time, I pretended like it was a pool, and I tried to dive deep. I wasn't looking where I was going, and the power of the current pushed me as I surfaced from my dive. I hit my head at the end of the ditch. I lost my energy. My senses started to dull. The only thing that I could feel was the cold of the water and the force of the current that kept me pinned alongside the ditch. I couldn't move or talk. I was scared. How did it all happen so quickly? I prayed to see someone coming outside to save me. I thought I was going to die.

I thought no one would come outside while it was raining, unless of course it was an emergency. Then, as if my prayers were answered, my nanny came outside to find her sweater, and she saw me lying there. She lifted me up immediately, and I felt relieved to be saved from the force of the current and the cold of the water that I thought was going to kill me. The doctor said that I hit my head so badly that I had to stay in the hospital for at least one week.

There is a big difference between how I am now and how I was then. The little girl that was inside me making me act selfishly and uncaring became a big girl with a lot of responsibility, someone who is caring and open minded. Since that time, I never go outside when it's raining. I even gave up my favorite place because of what happened to me there. Sometimes when I comb my hair where I hit my head, it still hurts. It's funny to think back on what happened in that place. Now, whenever it's raining, I think of that tiny place.

UPROOTED

Grace Roberts

When I want my legs to move, they remain completely still. Everything inside of me says, "go forward," but the outside world tells me not to move. I glance up at the tiny island across from the mainland. To anyone who may cast eyes upon me, I look like a fool. But there are no criticizing eyes or dirty glares watching my movement; the only eyes watching me come from my own rippling reflection in the murky water.

From where I stand, the stream doesn't seem so wide. I can observe the intricate patterns of the trees on the other side, and I can hear their rustling leaves. When I gaze back at the water, the current seems to surge with ferocious intensity. My fingers dance lightly on my thigh, where I imagine my fear has gathered.

It's something of a game for me: to jump over the rushing water and challenge the gods of nature has always quickened my pulse. In fact, I can't remember a time that this soil didn't coat my bare toes, or when I didn't hear the echo of the rumbling current. Some part of the thrill has since become a part of me. My blood flows like the stream itself.

In my fourteen years on this planet, I've experienced the darkest types of fear. It wasn't until I was tossed into foster care that I found a way to control it. I suppose that's why I spend so much time at the stream; it's the only place I have power over my conscience. Out here, there's no chance of finding a monster under the bed or a ghost in the closet. I've grown to love the isolation, and the wildness. Here, I don't have to stand up a little straighter or watch my language.

I take a slow and shaky breath, preparing my lungs for the possible rush of water. A bird flies overhead. As its squawk reverberates through the clouds, I lean back on my heels and wait. I wait for the trees to hush and for the water to settle. The second my breath slices through the silence, I sprint forward and soar over the water, which taunts me from below. In the three heartbeats that pass above the waves, I feel free, until I crash down on the other side.

The palms of my hands dig deep into the dirt. Thorns plunge themselves into my sweatpants. I grapple at the ground and hobble to a standing position. Turning back to the mainland, I study the crevice I've just leapt. I press my lips together in a tight line, but there's no stopping the smile welling somewhere inside of me.

I listen to the water swell for a moment. There's an old root jutting out of the bank and into the stream, so I rest my bare foot on the splintering wood. Water rushes past my ankles as I walk cautiously across the root. I hop onto the bank and yank my rain boots out of the mud. I look at them, and notice their color. Hot pink bathed in brown. Exhaling, I decide that it's time, and I trudge up the small hill leading to the path home. It's paved, and the black tar is soothingly warm on the soles of my feet.

* * *

A shrug slips off my shoulders when I see the house

ahead, knowing I can't go anywhere else. The smile inside of me has retreated. The cold mud has gone into my stomach. I hear the sliding glass door open quickly, and Cecelia appears on the back deck. She curses at me a few times, but I can't make out exactly what she's saying until I get closer.

"Utis!" she screams, glaring down at me. "Where have you been?"

I climb the deck steps before I respond and shake the last bits of mud from my boots. "I was at the stream," I reply flatly, which makes Cecelia scoff.

"All the dinner's in the trash," she grumbles at me. "If you want it, you'll have to dig it out."

By now, my feet are situated directly across from hers, and she's leaned down so close to my face that I can smell her breath. There's a sharp pang of alcohol, but no more than usual. I brush past her, and she stays in the same position until I'm completely inside.

The others are clearing the table, which is dangerously close to the door. My leg touches the corner, but I still manage to slide around it without any problem. The light fixture hanging from the ceiling swings back and forth silently, and I assume someone's head hit it. It's suspended by a busted chain and dangles at least six inches closer to the ground than it's supposed to, but I can't recall it ever being any other way.

I slip into the dimly lit dining room as quietly as possible, eyeing the others with a sort of uncertainty. They don't seem to notice my sudden presence, and they don't look up from their work when Cecelia slams the door shut. She puts her hands on her hips and begins her trek around the table. I feel her eyes burning into me, but I know better than to stop collecting silverware.

After a while, I feel her stare disperse, and my heartbeat settles a bit. I see her watching my foster brother now; he scrubs the table with a yellow-turned-brown sponge. "Do you think I'm going to spend the next week eating off a dirty table? Because at this rate, I think I might be." She runs a finger through the grime.

I wish I were courageous enough to snap that it'd be no different than any other day, but I've grown accustomed to holding my tongue. Here, I beat back the wild within me, because the wild in this house is not the kind you want to invite through the door. There's nowhere to escape Cecelia here should she do something extremely rash, but I don't have anything to hide. The wild is tucked away; only the stream has the power to pull it back out.

If I was afraid of my foster mother when I first arrived at her home, I've managed to eliminate the fear from my blood. Her words are always sharp, and they're usually encouraged by a lingering alcohol addiction. However, I've convinced myself that fear is only something if you make it something, so I simply decide that Cecelia isn't worth my emotions. As a result, everything gets locked up inside.

Although Cecelia's always had a dark side, it wasn't so obvious when our foster father, Robert, was alive. Since his recent passing, things have worsened, and the fridge's stock of alcohol has only increased. Robert was kind and down to earth; plus, he kept Cecelia away from her troublesome habits. All of their earned money went straight toward caring for us and securing our future.

Without him, the only thing we've got is a broken shell of a woman with smudged mascara and messy hair. She leans close to me when she's angry, so close that her wrinkles are as prominent as the sticks and roots in the stream. Today, the mud I've accidentally trailed into the house spurs her anger. Cecelia picks it up with her pointer finger and drags it across my cheek. I'm rooted to the ground, unable to pull myself from her; in the same way that the trees can't pull themselves from the stream. "Worthless piece of trash," she drawls, looking me up and down. "You belong on the street."

As she struts away to breathe down the backs of my foster siblings, I assure myself that although I belong somewhere else, it isn't on the street–it's at the stream. I have a place to belong, and I don't need anything else. I have a place to start fresh whenever I want. It is a place where something dangerous dwells, and something wildly free. And I believe that something is me.

WILD ICE

Grace Connolly

Kira sat on her window seat facing the lake, reading a copy of Vogue commandeered from her mother. Brown cardboard boxes secured with packing tape were strewn about her bedroom. Each had her name on it and her new address. She would miss this house, its small pink kitchen and its big front lawn surrounded by snooping neighbors who seemed to have nothing better to do than to stick their unusually long necks over the fence to see how the begonias were doing. But most of all, she would miss the lake.

The lake was her refuge. She would seek relief on hot days in its cool embrace and spend her days lounging on the sandy bank, one of her tabloids in hand, blocking out the world. When she swam in the murky depths, it felt like the water was alive. Kira's feet danced along the mud-caked bottom, stirring up sand and leaves and secrets. The secrets of her predecessors floated in the water like dead flies and discarded soda cans. They blended with the water, became the water and caressed Kira's body, wrapping her in a safe shield of thoughts and feelings, sharing with her a thousand private moments.

But now she wasn't in the lake stirring up secrets and feeling alive–she was in her room, packing up her belongings, moving to an apartment in a city she didn't want to go to, with an aunt she barely knew. Mom and

Dad "just needed to sort some stuff out." She stood up. Stretching, she yawned and cracked her back. Not packing really tired her out. She started down the white painted wood stairs on her way to the kitchen.

"Kiiira," a voice whispered, scraping the inside of her ears and sending a shiver down her spine. She looked around for the source but saw only the vacant ground floor. All of her mom's little knick-knacks were packed into boxes turning the once cozy living space into a skeleton. The vile taste of hurt, fear, and sadness bubbled up her throat but she quickly swallowed it back down.

"No," she scolded herself. "It doesn't matter. You don't care. There's nothing you can do." She kept walking, her cushioned footfalls echoing dully against the empty room.

"Kira. Kira. Kira," the voice continued, making her heart beat a million miles a second. Kira's eyes drifted to the glass sliding doors and out toward the lake. She walked cautiously over to the door and pressed her nose against the glass, her breath fogging it up. Something was moving. Kira pushed open the door and cold air punched her in the face. She drew a sharp intake of breath and bowed out onto the used-to-be-green grass. Her feet, clad only in lime green socks, moved up and down trying to stay warm against the cold New England winter.

"Kiiirrily," it said again, using her full name this time. The voice was cold and creepy, but also riddled with fear and the stale sound of betrayal. It slunk dejectedly over the small hill separating the house from the lake, her lake. A violent shiver struck Kira, and she wrapped her purple cardigan tighter around her shoulders. "What is this?" she asked herself.

"Why are you doing this?" she yelled, her sharp voice cutting through the wind. "Why now?" The wind stopped, and for a split second, Kira's world was silent.

Then the voice erupted with the vigor of a thousand serpents screaming in unison."Kira! Kira! Kira!" The screeching made her teeth ache.

Kira looked up. The lake was boiling. The water undulated like a pit of writhing snakes. When the sloshing liquid hit the frigid air it turned into ice—crazy, beautiful, wild ice. It pushed itself over the tall bank where Kira had spent many a day lounging in the sun and crawled up the side of the lawn whispering, "Kiiira," pain in each syllable. Tears welled up in her eyes and she tried to blink them away.

"I-I can't!" She gasped, tears staining her face. "It's not my fault! What do you want me to do?"

Kira backed up, not turning away from the ice until she was pressed up against the door. The ice followed, creeping up the little hill, pushing slowly but surely toward Kira's house and inevitably to her. It crawled up the door, sealing it in place and secured around her hand, freezing Kira in place. Dread pulsated through her veins.

"Please!" she whimpered. "Why are you doing this? What do you want me to do?" Hot tears dripped onto the ice, making a hisss on contact.

"Kiiira, Kiiira, Kiiira—stay."

ONE MAN'S FEAR

Nicholas Giroux

The cold flakes landed on the blackened tips of his fingers. Frigid air crept through his clothing and, like a bandit, stole his body's warmth from under him. Showing no sign of remorse, the flakes continued to engulf him in white, making him invisible from a distance, as if the snow had claimed him as a trophy. He could still feel it lurking in his wake. The thought of being followed, being spied upon from some unknown being drove him to the near point of insanity. For he was by himself, but he was almost sure that he wasn't alone.

He looked in every direction and saw nothing. All that he did see was a snowy haze acting like a veil as if meant to blind him, to ensure that a slow, painful death was near. But a sign of hope emerged from the cold. A silhouette formed in the distance making his mind race and his stomach churn. His eyes pooled as he ran and ran, nothing in his mind except to reach warmth. The impulse oozed out of him. The pure animal inside surfaced. It was there in his face. His eyes had hollowed and the bitter taste in his mouth became sweet.

As he approached the shadow it began slowly to become harder and harder to see until it vanished and he once again found himself watching the cold flakes of ice ravish his body and turn his thoughts against him. Was he going to die an insane man unsure of his life's meaning?

"No," he whispered under the constant wind rushing over his head, "No."

TRIANGLES

Mallory Campbell

He has pink hair.
Blonde, with a fuchsia mohawk.
I angle my camera, getting focused.
Trees are in micro.
His frame is in view.
I can see the position of the hands on his watches.
Three silver slant watches clank together
with every burdensome step.
They scream from the irritation of angles.
Jared runs toward me.
His eyes match the lightened sky,
but betray the forest.
Birds with floating feathers in hues of brown
find themselves in the crosshairs of my video.
Jared never looks at me.
He watches the moss along the sharp-tipped fence on both sides of him.
I feel the moss as a shadow growing over my heart.
His cheekbones are sharp.
Their shadow darkens a point at his torso and two more at his neck,
never reaching his uncontaminated eyes.
He wears a light denim vest with triangular pockets–
patches in the overcast of a black shirt.
His shirt, necklace, belt buckle, hair, and tattoos–

all are triangles.
Each is a small uneven, unconventional figure that represents him.
He runs to me, not seeing me.
Trees beckon me as to fill the void with their slight creaks.
Pops of light shine through the overbearing verdure that surrounds him.
The shadow doesn't touch any of the figures;
nor the hair that goes from dirty blonde, to bleach, to pink.
Jared is an understated free being who doesn't leave one feather behind, but flies.
Never once does he look toward the moss
now growing on my feet like a disease.
His presence of purity among the Taiga is a relief to those who travel here.
He illuminates the blood in the breeze by which he is not affected.
He seeks to break the fence and save those made sick by the forest of umber.
He runs by me; making the video immaterial.
Jared will remain pure and running.
I will stay here with a shadowy void growing on me
like moss on a fence–
a reminder of my impurity.

RUNNING IN A PACK

Matthew Gott

All I could hear was the faint touch of spike against ground. One after the other, they dug deep into the firm terrain and came out with strength. I could hear the breathing of the runners around me, all with different paces and equal power. I felt the ground sink beneath me in the short moment I stayed, and then I felt it push me back up, and forward. Those eighteen or so minutes in the woods were the most flawless moments of my life. Running in a pack, with five other men in unbearable pain, was the most tranquil I've ever felt. I felt the wind punish my face and I pushed through it.

I felt like I could do anything in those woods, that nothing could hold me down. I wasn't just running to finish with the best time or the best place, I was running to run. I wanted to feel the freedom, that step after step of full self-control. When we ran through those woods, we couldn't be stopped. The pack and I together felt closer to one another than anyone else and I felt like I could do anything, that I was free.

I remember Regionals this year so vividly. The team got off the bus, and it was near perfect conditions for running: cool enough so that you didn't sweat all the water off before the race, yet warm enough that I could feel my hands. There were meets when the sun drained the energy out of me and there were meets when the air I breathed in didn't feel like air at all, it felt like ice.

Going in, I was the most nervous I had ever been before a race. We felt enormous pressure as a team. Going to States was something my school had accomplished the previous seven years, but this year we found ourselves on the fringe. We were expected to be heading to New England's, and we didn't want to be the team with huge expectations that didn't make it. Injuries and freak events had hurt us all year and we just had to perform today.

After a good warm-up, I took to the line. The starter called "on your marks" and the inevitable silence began, that long silence, when everyone was nervous and everyone was ready. The gun split the air and we headed out as a pack of one hundred plus men, running into the woods, to be alone and experience the true feeling of the wild and the motivation to do as well as we could. The crowd noise murmured away as we went into the trees and all I could hear were men around me.

That was the beauty of this sport; I was more nervous than I had ever been only thirty seconds before, and then I felt free and at peace. On the line, every fan watched and I felt as if I were in a cage, yet when I got to those woods, I felt I had escaped. The trees stood still, and the men just kept running. Stepping and breathing, stepping and breathing. The woods during a cross-country race brought us freedom and let us all harness our wild sides.

I ran in a "passing pack," where a bunch of guys started out on pace and then built up to pass people in the second and third miles. I don't remember the middle at all but I remember how happy I was at the end when I found out I came in seventeenth with a PR. Getting that rank as a personal record didn't warrant a freakout type of happiness, just more this inner excitement, and I wanted to run around and high five everyone but instead maintained a relative calm of waiting to see how the team had done.

My dad knew whether we made States or not before they announced it and I saw a smile on his face, so I assumed we'd made it. The announcer said, "Seventh place, Mt. Ararat," and two claps resounded throughout the gym. I looked at Jake, the spiritual leader of the team, with his hands in his face. The rest of my teammates held open expressions on their faces—disbelief. We knew only the top six teams would move on, and I felt a profound sadness for them all.

The bus ride home was quiet and still, with the exception of my two friends and I, who had always run cross country for the fun and the feeling. We enjoyed that bus ride home. We laughed, we cried for happiness, and we loved every second of it because we knew, with seniors on our team and this being our last cross country season together, we might never have that chance to be wild again.

Being wild, at least in those woods, was letting go. It was not letting anything hold me down, allowing myself to be open and free. It made me realize the only thing entrapping me or keeping me down was myself. No one was imprisoning me, I was just imprisoning myself. When I hit those woods though, I had to allow myself to be free. I had to forget all my worries and let go of everything–then, only then, was I free to be wild.

THE BEAUTY OF THE BASSLINE

Ryan Freeman

Hundreds upon hundreds of people pack into the State Theatre, all for the same reasons–to let loose and live a little. The room is full of blinding lights and music loud enough to quell whatever stressors you may have that exist beyond the front doors. People are handing out free water and selling Red Bull for much more than it needs to be. The distinct smell of sweat, smoke, and stale beer fills the air–all scents that are terrible individually, yet combine to form the signature aroma of having a good time. The merch line is essentially nonexistent, but no one is worried–everyone will stop by after the show. People are packed together so tightly it's as if the crowd is a singular entity. The DJ up front has one of his earphone cups pressed to his ear, transitioning from one party anthem to another, in hopes of keeping the sea of fans moving. An MC shouts at the crowd, "Put your hands up!" even though everyone is doing it anyway.

The bassline shakes the floor and the kick drums threaten to cave holes in everyone's chest. These are the elements that keep everyone in sync–keeping the beat and providing danceable grooves. Wild, gritty synthesized noises may be screeching or wobbling, the type of thing that might make an out-of-touch generation ask, "They call this music?" Or they could be belting out an epic melody, the kind of progression that would even rival the emotion of classic gospel. Entrancing female vocals or samples taken from YouTube videos make appearances every now and then, and remixes of popular songs keep the floor thumping. Conversations that were once happening are no longer, as people resort to yelling to one another and screaming at every drop.

The crowd is comprised of people from all stages of life–young, old, middle-aged. You'll find "college bros" with their tank tops and reversed hats, "PLUR-head ravers" with their kandi bracelets and neon clothing, and people who are so new to the scene that they have no idea what's going on. The last kind are my favorite, actually, because they're typically the most open-minded and fun to watch. They're experiencing everything for the first time and it gives me the nostalgic feeling, remembering my first time and how absolutely culture shocked I was. One of the most amazing things is watching how everyone takes care of one another. This mostly goes for the "PLUR-heads."

PLUR is a code of conduct that means peace, love, unity, and respect, and it is taken extremely seriously among older ravers. It's warning people in the front of oncoming crowd surfers, checking on people who may be getting dehydrated, or just straight up looking after people who may have ended up too drunk or high to take care of themselves. Many people in the scene take it upon themselves to make sure everyone is safe and having a good time, because everyone is just looking to have a little fun–there's no reason to have it ruined by preventable incidents.

Part of the appeal of these events is the ability to shed who you are to the "outside world" and let yourself be free for a few fleeting hours. Leaving whatever problems or predisposed notions you have at the door is the key to having a good time. The "Rules of Dada," a list of funny quips by the respected Swedish duo Dada Life, dictates that one should never "bring your brain to a rave." This does not mean to act stupid or take enormous risks, but to stop calculating every move made and just "go with the flow." The "mature" and "unfun" accountant, or at least deemed so by his peers, could be the life of the party once he steps into the venue. The freedom of being able to lose yourself among possibly thousands of other people, all wishing to do the very same, is something that can simply not be compared to anything else I have ever been a part of. The idea of everyone coming together to lose their egos and simply become part of the crowd, indistinguishable from one another, is beautiful to me.

THE STRANGER

Zahro Hassan

People around here knew that it got dangerous at night. As soon as the sun went to sleep, everyone rushed home avoiding the dangers that would come about in the streets. I walked home through the darkness of the night, and a sense of fear began to grow inside me.

I regretted not getting a coat from home because my whole body was freezing. When my mother was alive, she used to force me to wear my coat. Every time I tried to sneak out of the house without one, she would run behind me to put a jacket on me, and she would chase me until I gave up. In those days, I never worried about anything. My mother made me feel proud of myself. She always told me how beautiful and smart I was.

The streets were vacant now, and a chilly wind began to below and send shivers down my spine. Everyone in the city was in the comforts of home except for those at the club. That place was always open till midnight. As I walked on the opposite side of the street from the club, I could hear the loud music booming from it.

I smiled and my teeth became cold as I worked to remember those beautiful moments with my mother. My smile faded when I heard footsteps behind me. I dared myself not to turn around and look behind me. I started to walk faster and crossed the street. The person behind me also crossed the street. I panicked and started to pray to God to protect me. Why was this person following me? Maybe this person who I refused to look at was going the same direction I was.

Then I looked back. It was a man who was barely an adult, probably an eighteen-year-old kid. He had brown curly hair and his eyes shone through the dark. He had his hand in his pocket and was busy on his phone. This reassured me a little bit and I crossed the street again in the direction of my house.

The stranger crossed the street again. He was following me. My heart did a double twist. I was definitely in danger. I wanted to run but knew that this person would outrun and catch me.

I could see my house in the distance. A bright light was shining through the window. It was almost a mile away.

Suddenly I saw a group of men laughing and telling jokes in front of an old apartment. They wore colors, black and red, representing their gang. This guy following behind me, I thought, was a part of this crew. But he was not wearing black and red like them. He was wearing a shirt and a tie. But maybe he was following me because he was the leader and was leading me toward them so they could torture me. So far, his crew couldn't see me approaching because it was night and there were trees in the way.

While I was thinking about how in the world I was going to escape the dangerous men ahead of me, the man grabbed me from behind and put his hands on my mouth to shush me if I screamed. I felt like my heart was going to come out of my throat because it was beating there, a million times a second. I turned around while the man's hand was still covering my mouth.

"Stay quiet if you don't want those guys to kill you," he said in a loud whisper.

I shook my head yes and prayed that he wouldn't do anything. He looked over my head to where the gang was and asked me to follow him.

I removed his hand from my mouth. "Umm, my house is this way," I said, pointing to the direction where the gang was. "You see that house behind the train tracks and these trees?"

"Come with me," he said dragging me by the hand. As he pulled me through the trees, I realized that he was leading me past the dangerous guys and the railroads tracks. We went on and on through the dark trees. They looked like gigantic monsters with a million hands and they stretched as far as my eyes could see. I turned and stared at the man leading me. I felt a sudden panic and pulled my hand away from his grasp. We had been walking for a while and I could see my house a couple of trees away.

The guy seemed surprised and stopped so he could face me.

"Umm, my house is over there, but thanks, I think I can walk from here," I said, backing away from him slowly.

"Wait, let me just make sure that nobody is there," he said, looking over my shoulder.

"It's fine, my house is literally right there," I said, pointing to my small white house, just ten feet away from us.

"I'll stand right here until you get there. Alright now, walk!"

I started walking toward my house and turned around to see him standing where I left him. He had his hands in his pockets and was staring at me.

I went inside. I felt the quietness of my house and caught my breath. Then I looked out the window. The stranger who saved me from the dangerous gang was walking away.

I turned the light in the living room and noticed how messy the house was. The dishes were dirty in the sink. My whole body ached. While I cleaned the house, I thought about the man. Why did he help me? I didn't even know his name.

THROUGH THE STORM

Faris Baziga

I went walking through the streets during a snowstorm. Houses, cars, and sidewalks were hidden by white cold ice. I wore sweatpants, a sweater, and a string-clothed hat. I had my Jordans on. I walked along Merrill Street, up on Munjoy Hill. No one was in the streets. It was foggy. You couldn't see anybody. I was trying to find the new apartment my family had moved to in the East End. The new apartment was about a fifteen-minute walk from where we used to live. The night seemed unending.

I kept moving through the same streets, yet the snow still dropped. Big snowflakes hit my eyes, and the coldness raised goose bumps all over my arms. The cold burned. I felt like going into a random apartment just to catch the warmth inside. I walked up the same block I had been through. When I had moved down Lafayette Street for the fourth or sixth time, I realized I had lost my way back home.

* * *

Home was back in Africa, where it was full of markets, people, and motorcycles. I loved sitting on the small front porch of our house. We had a little garden where we planted a few crops, such as tomatoes and avocados. I remember two big trees we had. One of them was called *muarbini.* It could treat forty illnesses. The other one was known as *mravumba*, and could treat skin diseases and headaches. My mom was the one who told me that the muarbini tree could treat the worst disease in Africa, known as malaria here. The smoke from burning the wood or bark of the *muarbini* could kill all the mosquitoes in one's house. Putting its leaves into a pot with water and drinking the liquid helped destroy malaria. I once tasted the *muarbini,* but it tasted sour, like green pepper, but worse than that. If you couldn't resist it, you could puke.

Near those trees, in my neighborhood, I loved playing soccer. Blocks bet money on games. My friend Tutu and I played a lot. I used to play as a defenseman or midfielder. We played eight-on-eight games. I knew most of my teammates well because we lived close to each other. My best friend Tutu played striker. During the weekends or on vacations, we wandered through the streets of Mumena and Kivugisa, where the sun shined upon us.

* * *

I grew even colder. I couldn't feel my fingers. I had to heat myself up by rubbing my hands together for friction. I kept moving through the snow, still wondering where my apartment was. At times, I thought I saw familiar buildings, but when I got closer to them my hopes died and the fear in me grew. I couldn't take it anymore. I asked a man for his phone to call my mom for directions.

The man was tall and he had covered himself in a long coat.

"Excuse me, sir, can I use your phone to call my mom?" I asked.

He looked at me and said, "No, I don't have a phone."

* * *

In Africa, I felt fear, too. It wasn't always sunny and safe. Sometimes it was worse than the snowstorm. Wild things had surrounded me, back when I lived on the banks of the Akagera River. I saw dangerous animals there: crocodiles and hippos, and some wolves. The harm they could cause was either injury or death. They were a threat to me, especially when I went to collect water in the morning. News could come back to us that someone had gotten caught by a crocodile and died, no remains found. That really scared me. Even worse, small and medium-sized snakes from a military camp that my family and I lived close to came to our house. Sometimes I stepped on the small snakes, killing them without even knowing it. I remember when a cobra snake was in our outdoor kitchen. It frightened my mom really badly. "Aaaaahhh!" she yelled, and then called my dad on his cell phone and one of my uncles who lived close to us. A few minutes later, they came to our house and told my mom and me to stay away from the kitchen. They used a machete and a metal bar to kill it.

* * *

The idea of death came to me when the coldness got to my feet. I couldn't feel my toes. That was the worst feeling ever. But in me I said, "I can do it. Let me just keep moving." And then I saw a kid about my age. He was a white kid, kind of big. He was dressed for the weather in a big jacket.

I asked, "Hey, there, do you have a phone I could use to call my mom?"

He replied, "No I don't, but there's a gas station across the street. You might find one there."

I felt relieved. I thanked him and walked fast to the gas station, where I met a lady who was polite and gentle. She let me use the phone. I dialed my dad's number, but I didn't get an answer. And then I called my mom's phone.

"Hello?" she said.

"Hello, Mom, it's me, Faris. I'm at 7-Eleven, and I'm lost," I said.

"What are you doing out this late at night?" she asked.

"Mom, I'm freezing. I've been out here looking for the house for two hours," I said.

"Well, walk straight up the street from 7-Eleven till you see Emerson Street, and turn left," she said.

"Thank you," I said.

She ended the call saying, "Get here quick. It's too dangerous outside."

* * *

It was way more dangerous in Africa, because of the witchcraft that occurred, day and night. We had to stay away from witches and evil spirits. Some people in America do not believe in witchcraft; they say they never believed in that voodoo stuff. But I do, because I've seen it. Witchcraft is used out of greed and selfishness, or to get back at someone, or to get wealth, love, and more. For example, you could find yourself at the same income level as someone else, but the day after some witchcraft you might find out that he or she had become rich out of nowhere.

Some witches contain more power than others. Some send evil creatures to carry out their power, such as a human bat. This scares other men and me because it is believed that it can rape any man it can catch. These spirits and witches had rules that should be followed to avoid their evil doings, and if not followed properly the wicked deeds could come back at you. The majority of people who use witchcraft are rich politicians and famous people who seek more than they have and do not think of the poverty and misfortune they cause the victims of their actions.

* * *

I finally got home and I felt really happy, at last getting to see my parents and my sister. But I was also angry that if I had only moved further out from where I was at first instead of making the same small circles, I could have reached our new apartment on my own. But still I felt relaxed and calm, and I headed to the shower. While in there I thought of my connections to my friends back in Africa. I thought, "If I die, or something bad happens to me, how would they know what happened?" It was pretty horrible to think about, but on the other hand the people I love most are with me, and living together in a country of peace and prosperity, where I know I am safe at all times. I took a glimpse out the window, and I saw the snow was still falling, but it looked soft. I thanked God that I made it home.

NUESTRA CAZA DE NOCHE

Eric Martinez Rodriguez

The day had gotten late and it was difficult to see. I left my house, walked across the grass, and climbed the nearby hill so that I could make a phone call to my *tia* Evangelina. I had called to see if my cousin's health had improved. Evangelina told me that they had taken her to the hospital, and that she was beginning to feel better. I heard relief in her voice and felt myself lean into the maple tree at my back, relieved too.

She continued to explain, but from the hilltop I saw the headlights of a car heading down the dirt road to my house. This was very strange, because almost no one visited us at our home in La Tecolota, much less at night. Our nearest neighbors were more than an hour away on foot in Montenegro. The car parked halfway down our driveway in front of the yard, keeping its distance from the house. I told my *tia* that I had to go. After hanging up, I could hear a few voices coming from the car, but I didn't recognize them.

Curious, I walked toward my house. I could see many shadows. Two of the figures were smoking. "*Buenas noches,*" I said to them.

Three adult voices replied, "*Buenas noches,*" and two smaller figures remained quiet. When I heard their voices I thought I might recognize one of them. One of the men who was smoking lit a lamp. It illuminated their faces and I realized I recognized many of them. They had come from El Pinar, a town named after the pine trees.

I invited them in and went to find my father. He was sitting in bed, reading his favorite book, *Almanaque*, which was full of curiosities and jokes. When he heard about our visitors, his face became serious. He put on his boots and went outside. While he spoke to the men I ate a few tortillas with cheese, waiting. After a short while, my father came into the room, and his face was alight with excitement. He told me we were going hunting.

My father and I spent our days working in the fields, and milking our cows Mariposa, Quesadilla, and Oscurana. But at night, we liked to go hunting. I began to prepare for the long night ahead, putting on my boots and changing into a darker shirt. I found my machete and gathered my flashlight, hat, and sweatshirt. Hunting was my father's favorite pastime. A coffee farmer by day, when night fell he would go hunting, often by himself, climb a tree and stay quiet for hours, waiting for the fast-moving *cotuza*. Dressed entirely in black, including a black *sombrero*, he almost always came home with an animal.

Maybe that is why we lived in the forest. Green hills, pines, maize fields, and sugarcane surrounded us. Leaving the suffocation of the city, he had moved us all far away and into the woods of La Tecolota, or "The Owl," as the place was known for the nocturnal birds living in the trees. He built our brick house near a mountain. Legend has it that this mountain had a tree that grew the best fruit–the sweetest oranges. You had to peel and eat them at the site of the tree itself. If you tried to take them with you, you would get lost on the mountain. I never looked for the tree myself, but I had heard of people who had found it.

A few others gathered and the adults began to plan out the hunt. The group was this: my dad and Nando, who were both excellent hunters. Nando fought in the civil war and lost four fingers on his right hand when a grenade exploded. My dad fought in the war too. They had known each other since they were boys. Then there was Gerson, who always had a cigarette in his mouth. Our fathers were friends. Antonio was really quiet and only spoke to Gerson. I didn't know him. Javier and José, their boys, talked and played in the mud while we began walking.

In the end, it was decided that my father and Nando would go one way and I would lead Gerson, Antonio, José, and Javier in another. Our meeting point would be in the valley at the grand *amate* tree. My father and Nando picked up their rifles and walked out into the darkness. We waited about fifteen minutes and then went a different way.

We hoped to find a deer. If we did, my family would eat for three days. We didn't expect to see any armadillos because we didn't bring any dogs with us. Dogs are experts at seeking them out in their caves. Maybe we'd hear a coyote, but I knew we would never see one. There was a story of a man from another village who came face to face with a tiger in those woods near the spring, *nacimiento del agua.*

We walked in a long line because the path was narrow. I was at the back behind the young boys, José and Javier, who were afraid of being left behind. I felt energized to be in the forest again. Everything was wet, from the rain that day, and I could smell the humidity moving between the trees. The air felt cold in my lungs. I felt a connection to these woods deep inside me. A nighthawk flew over us, but as we walked and walked we didn't see any other wildlife, only cows out to pasture. I wondered if maybe this was because we were a large group making quite a bit of noise.

We carried flashlights, hoping to catch the two little lights of an animal's eyes at the end of the beam. Oftentimes we would see rabbits, but we saw nothing. It was so dark. There were times where we heard strange sounds in the dry leaves, maybe rats, but how could we have known for sure? The most challenging thing about our night walk was that it was winter and the grass had grown tall and thick and was difficult to pass through. The brambles and thorns stuck in my skin like nails, scratched me, and took my blood. Our sweatshirts, jeans, and shirts ripped and pieces remained behind us in the forest.

We came across a spot on the trail where we saw many diverging paths. Gerson turned, suggesting we try a different route. Everyone agreed. I felt like he might be wrong for some reason, but I didn't want to be disrespectful and he seemed confident so I didn't say anything. We followed him, hoping to have better luck.

We came across a large swamp and had no choice but to cross it. It was deep and I almost lost my boots in its mud. The young boys followed in Gerson's and Antonio's boot prints, no longer laughing. We were all more serious, trying to remain quiet so as not to scare the animals. On the other side of the swamp, the brush was thicker. I did not recognize the forest around me, and the night grew even darker. The strange thing was that, bit by bit, the path began to disappear in front of us. I knew we had gone the wrong way.

Soon Gerson admitted his mistake. He didn't stop walking, though. Javier and Jose looked afraid. The night was nowhere near over, and we were far from home. We forgot about the hunt and concentrated on finding our way back to a route we knew. We came across a ravine and took great care on the slippery rocks and ledges so we would not fall into the deep rainwater-filled ditch below. We kept our eyes forward, hoping to see the light of my father's lantern. The only light we saw was that of the stars above. The stars' shine calmed me because they were so constant and sure of their place in the sky.

I looked down from the sky and saw a light far away through the trees. The light moved across the trees, and then dimmed. Gerson started making signs with his own flashlight, hoping to catch the other's eye. We knew it was my father. It was impossible for him to get lost in the woods. He knew them like the palm of his hand.

It was a relief to see his light, and soon he came into view. Finding him meant that everything was going to be all right because he always knew where he was. I liked that about him. My father wanted to complete our journey so he led us the final stretch to the *amate* tree. We sat on its enormous roots and rested. We talked over the night, lamenting that neither group had found an animal. Standing up to go home, my boots wet and stiff under me, I hoped that maybe we would find an animal on our way back.

We had been walking for a few moments when my father noticed a possum on the limb of a pine tree. These possums were known for eating our chickens, so my dad pointed and shot his rifle. Maybe he did this because we had had such bad luck on the hunt, or maybe just because he enjoyed using his rifle. The possum didn't fall immediately. It took its time and gripped the branch it stood on. When it fell we simply picked it up by the tail and looked at it. It was a female. We threw her to the side of the path and continued on toward home, tired from our long walk.

I had never gotten lost in those woods before, and I haven't since. Now, I live in Maine with my sister. There is deer hunting here, but you have to have a permit. Back home, you didn't have to ask permission. Everything was wild. I call my dad on the phone in La Tecolota and he asks me if I remember the woods there. I tell him that I do. I can still smell the wet fur of the catch, feel the night air in my chest, and the forest's heat on my skin.

THE FOREST OF THE RUNAWAYS

Molly Ruth Daley

Mona sat on the edge of a sturdy wooden chair, tapping her fingernails on the table in front of her. She could hear the rumble of her parents' snores in the next room. Her lungs felt constricted by the pressure of her minuscule world. The kitchen walls crept toward her and an insufferable sensation of claustrophobia set in. Wispy hairs on the back of her neck stood on end, and her cheeks were patched with angry, red blotches. Her skin crawled and her muscles tugged at her bones, urging them to move, to stand, to flee. She pushed herself away from the table and out of the chair. Her legs carried her out the back door. Barefooted, she ambled across dew-soaked grass, and through the gate that shielded her house from the outside–a world of harsh light, blaring sound, and pungent smell.

She unlocked the gate determinedly. Her senses embraced the thrilling stimuli beyond her fence with an eagerness that had lain idle within her for ages. She hiked up the swerving hill that loomed over her home. In the shadows of the hill, her house remained, rooted securely in place. Steely gray clouds hung heavily overhead, obscuring her view of the top of the hill. Every few beats, her heart longed for her home below, and the comfort it provided. But the air around her was cool, and her legs continued to propel her purposefully away from her comfort and closer to her future, the mysterious unknown.

The clouds rose with her as she came to the crown of the hill. Her pounding heart was no longer ailed with bereavement, but instead was preoccupied with the rapid pace that adrenaline generated. She stood valiantly at the hilltop, and looked down on her world as she'd known it. It was a dreary world of small houses with slanted roofs, lined up like soldiers in crisp uniforms. She saluted them, and they bowed in somber response.

One house, painted a stark white, held the fragile lives of Mona's parents, protected by black shingles overhead, and gray shutters aside hazy windows. She watched them dawdle jadedly about their cramped abode, stoking a stiflingly hot fire and pouring bland porridge into yellow and orange plastic bowls. Their routine made her stomach ache with vexation, and she felt sickened by their apathy.

Mona shook her head and took a greedy swallow of fresh air, grateful to be high above the dead, stagnant air that rested listlessly in her mundane house. Air inhaled and exhaled repeatedly by the same people who thought the same thoughts. Air that held the uninspiring words of tired humans content with perpetual exhaustion.

"Boy," she sighed into the chilly air that nipped at her ears and flushed her cheeks. "I sure am glad I got out of there when I did." Only the wind whistled in return.

"Boy!" Mona called louder into the empty air. "If I'd stayed in that terrible house another day I might have fallen into permanent sleep, just like the rest of them!" But once again, no one gave a response, or acknowledged her thought, or even her existence. With a frustrated pout she rose to her feet and began to wander the world she had yet to explore.

Through thorny bushes and wiry branches Mona trekked all day, kicking at stones that jutted from the blanket of decaying leaves underfoot. She tucked frizzy strands of hair behind her ear to keep them from catching on prickly vegetation. The sun had risen, dissipating the fog and brightening the previously gray sky. Streaks of magenta and tangerine stretched across the horizon, textured like an exquisite oil painting. Puffy clouds of a silvery white floated swiftly across the sky, spurred by the breeze.

She followed the flaxen-colored orb overhead as she continued her hike through the rugged forest, each step taking her further and further from all she knew. She blazed new trail over untrammeled soil and jumbled brush. Each shrub and canopy glimmered and shone brilliantly, a kaleidoscope of hunter greens and emeralds. The leaves fluttered and swayed, executing a beautiful and effortless dance. As the hours passed, the sun began to follow her on her solitary adventure. Then behind her, it warmed her hair and back.

Mona's stomach was plagued by hunger, as she had skipped her morning porridge and had eaten nothing since. She had loathed the repetitive, tasteless meal every day it had been served to her, but suddenly she missed it terribly. As the sun fell beneath the tree line, she began to forage for berries and edible plants. The dimming light made it difficult to find a single morsel.

Before long the moon had nudged the sun from

the darkening blue sky, and the overwhelming blackness of night held her. What little light there was emanated from the luminescent crescent and the glittering stars above her. She meandered with hindered vision through the wild forest surrounding her. She'd relished her freedom, but loneliness began to gnaw at her ankles.

Mona felt a heavy tear collect in the corner of one eye, but then she encountered the edge of a clearing, in which the company she yearned for sat in a lopsided circle.

Countless children were grouped around a small pile of glowing embers, radiating just enough heat to ensure warmth, but not so much to suffocate or smother the assembled gathering. The children were engaged in conversation that seemed to rivet them, as they did not notice Mona hide behind a thick tree trunk. She strained to hear the words that slipped so effortlessly from their mouths. Curiosity forced her out from her hiding spot, and she approached the circle.

"I'm Mona," she called gently to the children, nervous to interrupt their intense focus. Each of them turned to her, with wide eyes. Their ears seemed to stand up like an animal's and point in her direction.

"Welcome," the children greeted her. She was almost surprised they spoke her language, so amazed was she that they were there at all in this deep forest. Two of them scooted eagerly apart, making space for her, the newcomer. She joined the circle as one of the children handed her a cup of water and a leaf filled with nuts and berries.

"What brought you here, Mona?" a small boy

asked.

"I ran away," she replied as she stretched her muddy feet toward the fire. She felt herself fall easily into the otherworldly atmosphere created in the hammock of the woods, the fire, and the ring of children. "I was getting tired, you see, and I didn't want to fall asleep. My parents sleep soundly on their feet, all day long, day after day, and they just don't seem to care at all!"

The children nodded sympathetically, and murmured their congratulations for escaping such a lethargic world.

"You'll like it here, Mona. We don't sleep," said a young girl with deep brown eyes.

"We can't sleep," another child chirped in a joyful tone. "If we do, monsters may encroach on our glade, or flesh-hungry beasts, or even worse, the slumbering zombies that are our parents!"

All the children gasped then, in horror at the thought of such savages entering their virginal clearing, untouched by monsters, beasts, or parents. Mona saw that it was all theirs. A small world in which they had settled an intimate community of their own. The thought of an intrusion hurt their hearts. But the lack of security in the clearing made her heart ache as it had on the hill.

"We must stay awake to protect ourselves and each other. We must stay awake to survive!" the same child added, when the frightened exclamations had ceased.

Mona shifted nervously, worried at the possibility of such monstrosities lurking in the shadows. Dead leaves crackled with her every move and sparks roared up in the fire as a night breeze blew in as though a giant set of bellows stirred the wickedness there.

Her mind flooded with thoughts of home. Yes, it was abhorrent. The conversation was a bore; all the stories to tell had been told. When words were spoken, they were spoken softly, as not to disturb the unnerving peace that enveloped the cozy prison. It was an absolute horror! But, it was also safe. Here, a black-shingled roof, clean clapboard walls, or dove grey shutters did not protect the clearing of runaway children.

"It doesn't seem to be very safe here," Mona noted, feeling her throat tighten as she spoke. She did not want to insult this welcoming group of children, or their home, or their lifestyle, but it did frighten her. It had been a long, exhausting day, and she was much too fatigued to hide her emotions, even from strangers.

"Oh, it isn't," a clever boy stated matter-of-factly, shrugging his shoulders. A wide and charming smile spread across his young face. "It's very wild."

"Mona," a girl said in a pacifying tone, rolling her eyes at the boy, "he was not always this composed and confident. He was just as fearful and apprehensive as you when he first found us. Perhaps even more so! But, do stay with us. You will change."

"It's hard to wake up from comfortable slumber, and stay awake in this intimidating world at first," the small boy said, more softly, defending all of the children who had been scared upon arriving in the clearing. "It's simply terrifying to realize the dangers that exist outside of your picket fence. But you can't stay locked up forever."

Mona nodded, absorbing the knowledge and advice of her new friends.

"Mona," the young girl said, "soon you will appreciate the possible dangers of this unpredictable life we lead. Fear comes in handy for staying awake."

And with that, the children stared intently into the dwindling fire, and once again their voices crackled in the blackness surrounding them. Their long orange shadows ran up the trunks of trees and into the night.

WE WERE NOT WOLVES

Kaitlyn Knight

Placed among faces
with which I'm acquainted,
I find a time
when I was wild in a pack.

The sun rested and lent
the earth to its cooling brother.
That blind eye looked down on
five wolves, females,
before our prime.
The day was spent in celebration,
as was the night. Paws imprinted soft dirt.
Headlong we raced, young tongues lolling,
youthful eyes absorbing the moon-drowned road ahead.
Crouched behind bushes we lay in waiting.

We waited for the light-filled eyes of our prey,
speeding ever closer until
our battle anthem rose behind us.
We charged, pelts glinting ethereal dances to the sky.
The car belted an energetic approval.
Startled by the noise, we fled,
only to return to the hunt later.

We were not wolves.

Yet wild with our dim dances beside rural roads,
not to be remembered, nor found again.

Alone. Eyes glint only dimly,
darkened orbs that distract from keen teeth.
Precautioned people skirt left, right.
I crave only the life I live, with the moon and myself.
Being a wolf, pelt dancing. Being a girl, teeth clenched.

ASTRIFEROUS

Alicia Thurston

"Fishnets," was all the scraggly, doddering woman said
on Thursday night.
Her mouth twisted, slashed into a smile,
the ridges of them beginning to shrivel.
"Fishnets," she'd said again and again and again,
whispering until even the silence had become annoyed
to such a point, it began
casting her voice back to her, to fill its absence.
For she mustn't notice that it too had left.

"Fishnets," drawled the midnight sky,
turning in and in and in,
rolling head over heels, for all the people below.

A few more fishnets for Friday, Saturday,
and Sunday too.
Fishnets, until the meaning of the word had left her
mouthand all that remained
was the implantation of the letters on the soaking ridge
of her tongue,
in the far back of the cavern,
at the very apex of her throat.

In wake of her word, languages arose,
like planets in the void, or

jutted landscapes on the Earth below.

Languages that the woman herself could not speak,
but somehow knew.
Like the bright blue plastic net within her hands,
which left behind slivers of parted skin and speckles of
deep red ash.

“Fishnets,” cawed the woman Tuesday night, shambling
down to the cusp of the waterline,
ankles shuttering
and clasped by the wind that breached them,
hands curled far too tight,
around the light dipped mesh.

Taunting the damp sand with the horizon of her toes,
she stood,
a smirk blossoming across the field of her face.

She raised her arms, up and up and up,
cast the net over the illuminated casket in the sky,
ignored the shrieks of stars and lamentations of wind
and all the protests that were suddenly below her.
When the other side returned
she clasped it, pulled and pulled and pulled
until the moon had crumbled from the sky
and fallen to the lake below.

She continued on, trailing for a few more steps
into the water,
pulled once more, again and again and again

dragged that beast upon a shore
stared on as the dollop began
to swallow the grains of sand on the bed below it.

She turned her head from side to side
admiring her works done. The sky twirled on,
the stars scratched and scratched.
The moon remained upon the shore,
swallowing sand, drawing it into its heaving chest,
tendrils of light fleeing from its edges,
scorning the distant sky.

The woman went to the moon wrapped in fishnet.

The newfound child placed her hand upon its forehead,
smiled, and spoke:

"It's good to see you, old friend.
How about we speak again?"

EPILOGUE

Henry Spritz

"Who are you? Please, tell me who you really are, because I know I've met you before, and I'm almost certain I know when. But please, tell me."

"You really can't remember me?"

Kenny Lane looked up and saw sadness, pure, unavoidable sadness etched so audibly across the man's face, that he bit back a breath. And when he replied, his breath came out in a whisper. "No."

"It doesn't really matter, it wasn't really important, but what I told you, I mean, what I should tell you in something of great importance, a lesson that I could never have taught."

"And that is, sir?"

"Sometimes our idols do not always live up to their standards."

"Yes, that is true, sir, that is true, sir, very important. But if you'll excuse me, I think its time I left for home."

"Yes, yes of course, it is getting late. Tell your family to have a happy Thanksgiving."

"I'll do that, thank you, sir." Kenny Lane turned, and began to walk down the dusty dirt road that lead from the park into the heavily wooden trail that weaved behind the town, but suddenly turned as the man called after him.

"Oh, by the way, I'm sorry we couldn't figure out

how we knew each other, quite sorry to waste your time."

Kenny Lane smiled, he waved his hand, as if to dismiss some unseen trouble. "It's fine, sir, thank you anyways. I'm sure it will come to you."

And then he continued his walk, until his figure had fully disappeared among the heavy oaks, his footfall fading into the distance until all that could be heard was the cluttering and shivering of leaves on their branches.

The man stood, walking over to the apple tree in the center of the park, he was alone now, the schoolyard abandoned of any remaining children. The park was silent and still, like some massive dormant creature, just about to go into hiding once more. The man glided his hand across the rough stripping of bark, shedding the leaves like snowflakes off a cloud, gliding to the forest floor.

"You know," the man whispered, his face a plane of angles and shadows. "We're not too different, both of us stripped of our opportunity in the peak of our wisdom and glory. But you know," the man choked out his final words, "sometimes the time just comes, and you know you must leave."

He turned, his figure briefly silhouetted against the evening sun, and then with a flash of crimson, searing bright in the dazzling setting sun, the leaves around his feet flying in to the heavens, one last chance to fly, he was gone. Slowly the leaves settled again on the ground, and the park that no one truly knew was still once more. And the setting autumn sun sank peacefully into the blue curved horizon at the edge of the world, until nothing was left, save a half forgotten memory that lingered in the air.

* * *

It was warm out, and the slowly sinking sun brought light to the valley. And beneath the sloping hills leading up to the port, the large cargos ships were steaming off into the pink sky, their horns blowing long calls on the twilight air. A boy and his friends ran down to the docks, a fifteen-minute ride by car, but only a mere ten on the legs of an eight-year-old boy. They would sit on the docks, the old piers warm and sturdy beneath their bare feet, the crowds gathering at the chop ends in a throng to glimpse the vessels depart, waving bandanas and handkerchiefs, a sea of bobbing fedoras and teary-eyed mothers, all silently screaming the same thing in their minds, caught on their breath.

"Back! Come back! Come back home!"

And they would wave to the vessels as they limped away, churning the seas to foam and salty wake, teasing the crossing gulls with their flags and poles, drawing them behind their sterns like moths hovering above a flame as they danced above the waves, dodging through the white spray and up, up onto the masts of the ships. They too seemed to turn back and call out toward the shrinking shoreline.

"Back! Back to the home where we belong, we will be back one day, one day!"

* * *

It was a quiet night, and soft breezes carried away all traces of the day's rain off into the pink sky. The road was quiet, the tall pines swept shadows across the long tar stretch, winding and eventually, disappearing into the approaching night. Headlights, and the whine of an engine receded into the distance, punching holes of light in the forest wall.

The late day glow alit upon a small tollbooth, a ticket box, and a tired man, worn by the day's incredible slowness in its unimaginable haste. He sighed in his sleep, his beard was untidy, and his face unshaven, but the small bag of change held tightly in his large hands promised more than just that, and because of it, for the first time in months he slept easily and soundly.

When he woke on the new day, his eyes fluttering and heavy with sleep, the first rays of sun had already entered the sky and warm morning air was alive with the chatter of the crickets in the tall grass. The little thrushes of spring perched on the telephone pole, bouncing and bobbing through the air like boats on the endless sea.

The man knew it was time to leave, but couldn't, trapped in the peacefulness, the serenity, and the quiet; they were precious to him, those things, precious and rare, and too often he found himself missing the lazy days of summer when he was a child. For a brief moment, he harbored an overwhelming desire to run off into the woods and leave behind it all. He shook his head, put up his feet, smiled, and he waited, waited for what he wasn't sure, he simply waited.

He sketched the birds chirpings on the wires, he listened to the radio in the little tollbooth, classical, then blues, then sports, then silence, he walked barefoot in the little stream off the side of the highway, his pants rolled up, the cold water rushing from the backs of his legs all the way to the great blue ocean. He ate, little sandwiches his wife made him, he drank, orange juice from a little thermos, orange on white, like the sun on a snowy day. He watched, as large swathes of clouds rolled across the great blue canyon of the sky. And, of course, he waited.

It came around two o'clock, when the heat waves were rippling and the sweet smells of the fast approaching summer filled the air. It turned the blossoms to blooming, the birds to rejoicing, and the water to sing a melody sweeter than honey. It came. And the man knew, he saw, off in the distance, the faint outline of a wiry man, faint brushstroke silhouetted against the horizon.

The man smiled, watching as the stranger became more prominent. He was tall, the man in the tollbooth could tell that much, and thin, and he walked on the side of the road with a stride of importance, but also with the unmistakable walk of defeat. He carried no extra belongings. The man approached, his legs tall and thin, his arms lean and wiry, his face dusted by the rises of a thousand roads. His boots were worn to the crop, faded leather on ancient tar, the feet seemed to beg to go on, drawn into the ever receding horizon, a trophy that could never be won, but that could always be sought.

"Hello," the man stepped out from the booth, wiping his hands of his long work overalls. Squinting into the sun's glare, the tall man stepped forward, his weather-beaten face filled with a thousand stories the man knew he would never hear, nor understand.

"Hello." The tall man stood; still, but unmoving. Still.

"What brings you to these parts?" The toll man smiled, sitting down in his little box.

"Oh, it's a very long story and I'm sure I wouldn't bore you with it. Yes, it's very long, and very sad, and meant for another time."

The toll man gestured for him to begin the tale, but the tall man waved him off. "Please," he smiled wistfully and with melancholy, "there's a reason I was walking away from it."

The toll man nodded, "We all have our stories, and some are best left untold. Or at least we ought to leave out the middle parts."

They stood in silence for a minute, tuning in to the outside world, the birds, the wind, the water.

The tall man sat. And then they both waited, in silence, thinking over thoughts that would never be shared.

"Well, I best be going."

The tall man stood, stretching his gaze into the distance. "It was nice meeting you."

"Where will you go?" The toll man leaned forward, stretching out into the shadows.

"Oh, wherever the wind takes me, I never seem to have trouble finding a home." He smiled, "It's funny, every time I think I've found the place I want to live, then I remember, there is no place I can truly ever settle down, I'm too restless I suppose, and so maybe I'm never meant to, settle down you know. Maybe the road is the place I'm meant to be."

"Well, I'll see you then. I'll always be here," the toll man gestured ahead, into the road. "I'll always be here, waiting in my booth, in the road, so when you walk past, make sure you stop in and say hello."

The tall man nodded, smiling but also more serious than the toll man would ever suspect.

"I'll be around." And he was off again, walking down the road, his way lit by the huge sinking sun glinting through the thick forest wall. The toll man watched him until he disappeared from sight.

SELECTIONS BY GENRE

FICTION

NONFICTION

POETRY

Acknowledgments

The Telling Room would first like to acknowledge the following individuals and organizations, who made this book possible: Patty and Cyrus Hagge, Donald Sussman and Chellie Pingree, David and Sandi Whiston, the Harold Alfond Foundation, Anonymous, the Margaret E. Burnham Charitable Trust, the Virginia Hodgkins Somers Foundation, the Davis Family Foundation, the Old Bug Light Charitable Foundation, and the Jane B. Cook Charitable Trust. Thank you for your support. Without you, these stories and poems would remain scattered, unseen, and unfelt.

Thanks so much to Heather Davis for assembling the original ideas and language from which we could run with the "wild" theme. Her words form the Introduction to this book, and helped launch and propel the theme along all year. The pieces here began in Telling Room workshops, inschool residencies, yearlong writing projects like the Young Writers & Leaders program, Young Emerging Authors fellowship, and Young Authors Group, and through our annual statewide writing contest. Countless teaching artists, writing coaches, staff members, interns, and volunteers, who are always the engine by which The Telling Room hums, developed their work in these programs. We thank them all with huge high-fives.

Thanks so much to the parents and teachers who supported these young authors, and encouraged them to share their work. Please keep doing so—let us know if your schools, libraries, or bookstores are ever out of stock!

We would also like to thank the fabulous, hard-working editorial crew who met weekly through the bleak, endless winter months around The Telling Room's borrowed fifth floor conference table to discuss, dissect, reconstruct, and arrange the stories and poems for this collection. Emerald Stewart, Taryn Brennan, Abigail Chance, Rose Heithoff, and Molly McGrath formed the committee, and sat elbow-to-elbow with the student authors, discussing the high points of editorial content and development. This committee reached out to be sure all of the authors engaged in the revision process: the writing is certainly finer for it.

A special mention goes to RandeeSue Allen, who wrangled an impromptu editorial meeting with four students at Scarborough Middle School, and to Erin Bartnett and Allison Strausberg for their pinch-hitting and perfect pitch editing on a couple key narratives in the book.

Huge thanks to the rest of our production team: to The Beehive Design Collective in Machias for donating their incredible cover illustration; to Andrew Griswold for his brilliant layout and cover design; and to Walch Printing for gluing it all together.

Lastly, and mostly, thanks to these young authors. Our wildest applause is reserved for you.

About The Telling Room

The Telling Room is a nonprofit writing center in Portland, Maine, dedicated to the idea that children and young adults are natural storytellers. Focused on young writers ages 6 to 18, we seek to build confidence, strengthen literacy skills, and provide real audiences for our students. We believe that the power of creative expression can change our communities and prepare our youth for future success.

We serve those who are reluctant to write as well as those who already identify as writers, including: children and young adults who are a part of Maine's growing community of immigrants and refugees, those with emotional and behavioral challenges, students struggling in mainstream classrooms, homeschoolers enthusiastic to join a creative community, and passionate young writers who need additional support beyond what their schools are able to provide. To learn more, please check us out online.

Our fun, innovative programs enlist the support of local writers, artists, teachers, and community groups. At our downtown writing center we offer free afterschool workshops and tutoring, and host field trips for school groups from all over Maine. We also lead workshops at local schools and community organizations; bring acclaimed writers to Maine to give public readings and work with small groups of students; publish bestselling anthologies of student work and books like this one by our young authors; and carry out community-wide storytelling projects and events.

www.tellingroom.org